Following the Star

Solo Christmas Carol Arrangements

for Unaccompanied Violin

Myanna Harvey

Cover Image: The Miriam and Ira D. Wallach Division of Art, Prints and Photographs: Picture Collection, The New York Public Library. "Veselé Vánoce!" Guth, Zdenek (Artist) The New York Public Library Digital Collections. http://digitalcollections.nypl.org/items/510d47e3-4ab9-a3d9-e040-e00a18064a99

CHP392

©2020 by C. Harvey Publications All Rights Reserved.

www.charveypublications.com - print books
www.learnstrings.com - PDF downloadable books
www.harveystringarrangements.com - chamber music

Following the Star

Solo Christmas Carol Arrangements

Myanna Harvey

Table of Contents

	Title	Page
1.	**We Wish You a Merry Christmas** (Traditional English)	2
2.	**Good King Wenceslas** (Traditional European)	4
3.	**Carol of the Bells** (Mykola Leontovych)	5
4.	**O Tannenbaum; O *Christmas Tree*** (Traditional German)	6
5.	**What Child is This** (Traditional English)	8
6.	**O Come All Ye Faithful** (John Francis Wade)	10
7.	**Pat-a-Pan** (Bernard de la Monnoye)	12
8.	**Away in a Manger** (Traditional German)	14
9.	**Angels We Have Heard On High** (Traditional French)	16
10.	**O Come, O Come Emmanuel** (Latin Plainchant)	18
11.	**Up on the Housetop** (Benjamin Hanby)	20
12.	**Lo, How a Rose E'er Blooming** (Michael Praetorius)	22
13.	**Deck the Halls** (Traditional Welsh)	24
14.	**Fum, Fum, Fum** (Traditional Catalan)	26
15.	**Jingle Bells** (James Pierpont)	28
16.	**God Rest Ye, Merry Gentlemen** (Traditional English)	30
17.	**The First Noel** (Traditional French)	32
18.	**We Three Kings** (John Henry Hopkins)	34
19.	**Silent Night** (Franz Gruber)	36
20.	**Behold That Star** (Thomas Talley)	38
21.	**Coventry Carol** (Traditional English)	40
22.	**Hark, the Herald Angels Sing** (Felix Mendelssohn, William Cummings)	42
23.	**Joy to the World** (Lowell Mason)	44
24.	**The Holly and the Ivy** (Traditional English)	46

Following the Star

We Wish You a Merry Christmas

Trad., arr. M. Harvey

Following the Star: Solo Christmas Carol Arrangements for Unaccompanied Violin

©2020 C. Harvey Publications All Rights Reserved.

Good King Wenceslas

Trad., arr. M. Harvey

Carol of the Bells

M. Leontovych, arr. M. Harvey

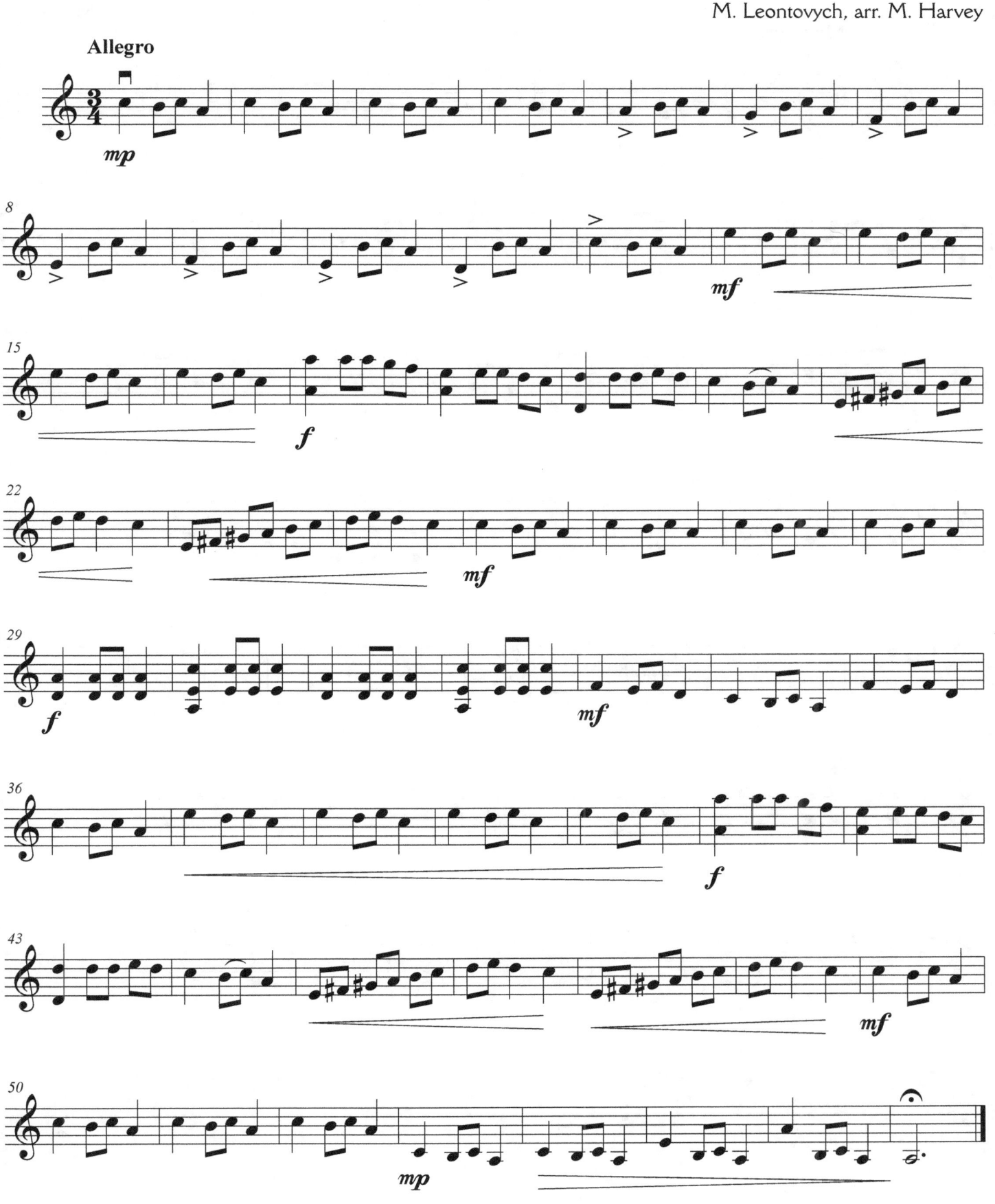

O Tannenbaum (*O Christmas Tree*)

Trad., arr. M. Harvey

Following the Star: Solo Christmas Carol Arrangements for Unaccompanied Violin

©2020 C. Harvey Publications All Rights Reserved.

What Child is This

Trad., arr. M. Harvey

Following the Star: Solo Christmas Carol Arrangements for Unaccompanied Violin 9

O Come, All Ye Faithful

J. Wade, arr. M. Harvey

Following the Star: Solo Christmas Carol Arrangements for Unaccompanied Violin   11

©2020 C. Harvey Publications All Rights Reserved.

Pat-a-Pan

B. de la Monnoye, arr. M. Harvey

Following the Star: Solo Christmas Carol Arrangements for Unaccompanied Violin

©2020 C. Harvey Publications All Rights Reserved.

Away in a Manger

Trad., arr. M. Harvey

Following the Star: Solo Christmas Carol Arrangements for Unaccompanied Violin

15

©2020 C. Harvey Publications All Rights Reserved.

Angels We Have Heard on High

Trad., arr. M. Harvey

©2020 C. Harvey Publications All Rights Reserved.

O Come, O Come Emmanuel

Latin Plainchant, arr. M. Harvey

Following the Star: Solo Christmas Carol Arrangements for Unaccompanied Violin

Up on the Housetop

B. Hanby, arr. M. Harvey

Following the Star: Solo Christmas Carol Arrangements for Unaccompanied Violin

Lo, How a Rose E'er Blooming

M. Praetorius, arr. M. Harvey

Following the Star: Solo Christmas Carol Arrangements for Unaccompanied Violin

Deck the Halls

Trad., arr. M. Harvey

Following the Star: Solo Christmas Carol Arrangements for Unaccompanied Violin

Fum, Fum, Fum

Trad., arr. M. Harvey

Following the Star: Solo Christmas Carol Arrangements for Unaccompanied Violin

Jingle Bells

J. Pierpoint, arr. M. Harvey

Following the Star: Solo Christmas Carol Arrangements for Unaccompanied Violin

©2020 C. Harvey Publications All Rights Reserved.

God Rest Ye Merry Gentlemen

Trad., arr. M. Harvey

Following the Star: Solo Christmas Carol Arrangements for Unaccompanied Violin

©2020 C. Harvey Publications All Rights Reserved.

The First Noel

Trad., arr. M. Harvey

Following the Star: Solo Christmas Carol Arrangements for Unaccompanied Violin

33

We Three Kings

J. Hopkins, arr. M. Harvey

Following the Star: Solo Christmas Carol Arrangements for Unaccompanied Violin 35

Silent Night

F. Gruber, arr. M. Harvey

©2020 C. Harvey Publications All Rights Reserved.

Following the Star: Solo Christmas Carol Arrangements for Unaccompanied Violin

Behold That Star

T. Talley, arr. M. Harvey

Following the Star: Solo Christmas Carol Arrangements for Unaccompanied Violin

Coventry Carol

Trad., arr. M. Harvey

Following the Star: Solo Christmas Carol Arrangements for Unaccompanied Violin

©2020 C. Harvey Publications All Rights Reserved.

Hark, the Herald Angels Sing

F. Mendelssohn, W. Cummings,
arr. M. Harvey

Following the Star: Solo Christmas Carol Arrangements for Unaccompanied Violin

©2020 C. Harvey Publications All Rights Reserved.

Joy to the World

L. Mason, arr. M. Harvey

Following the Star: Solo Christmas Carol Arrangements for Unaccompanied Violin

The Holly and the Ivy

Trad., arr. M. Harvey

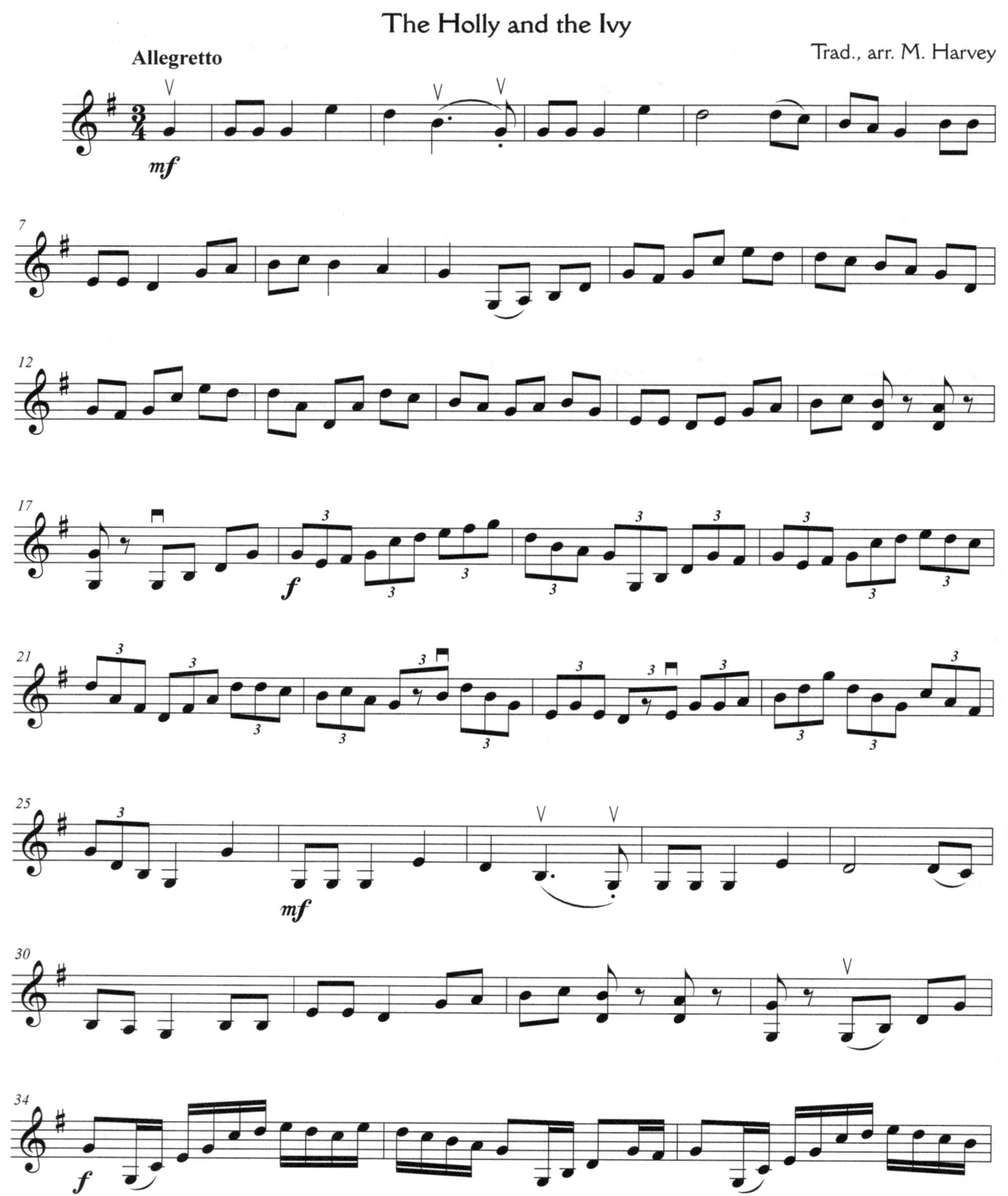

Following the Star: Solo Christmas Carol Arrangements for Unaccompanied Violin

You Might Also Like:

Fiddles on the Bandstand: Fun Duets for Two Violins
Book One

all duets arranged by Myanna Harvey

Table of Contents

Title
1. The Entertainer (Scott Joplin)..................
2. Take Me Out to the Ball Game (Albert Von Tilzer)..................
3. Yankee Doodle (Traditional)..................
4. The Stars and Stripes Forever (John Philip Sousa)..................
5. El Jarabe Tapatio; *Mexican Hat Dance* (Traditional)..................
6. Overture to *William Tell* (Gioachino Rossini)..................
7. America the Beautiful (Samuel A. Ward)..................
8. I'm a Yankee Doodle Dandy (George M. Cohan)..................
9. Jeanie with the Light Brown Hair (Stephen Foster)..................
10. My Country, 'Tis of Thee (Traditional)..................
11. Drill, Ye Tarriers, Drill (Charles Connolly)..................
12. Maple Leaf Rag (Scott Joplin)..................
13. Over There (George M. Cohan)..................
14. Simple Gifts (Traditional)..................
15. The Washington Post March (John Philip Sousa)..................
16. Let Me Call You Sweetheart (Leo Friedman)..................
17. The Star Spangled Banner (John Stafford Smith)..................
18. Funiculì, Funiculà (Luigi Denza)..................
19. You're a Grand Old Flag (George M. Cohan)..................
20. Summer, from *The Four Seasons* (Antonio Vivaldi)..................
21. Armed Forces Medley (Various)..................
22. Pomp and Circumstance March No. 1 (Edward Elgar)..................
23. Overture to *The Barber of Seville* (Gioachino Rossini)..................

CHP367
$9.95   www.charveypublications.com

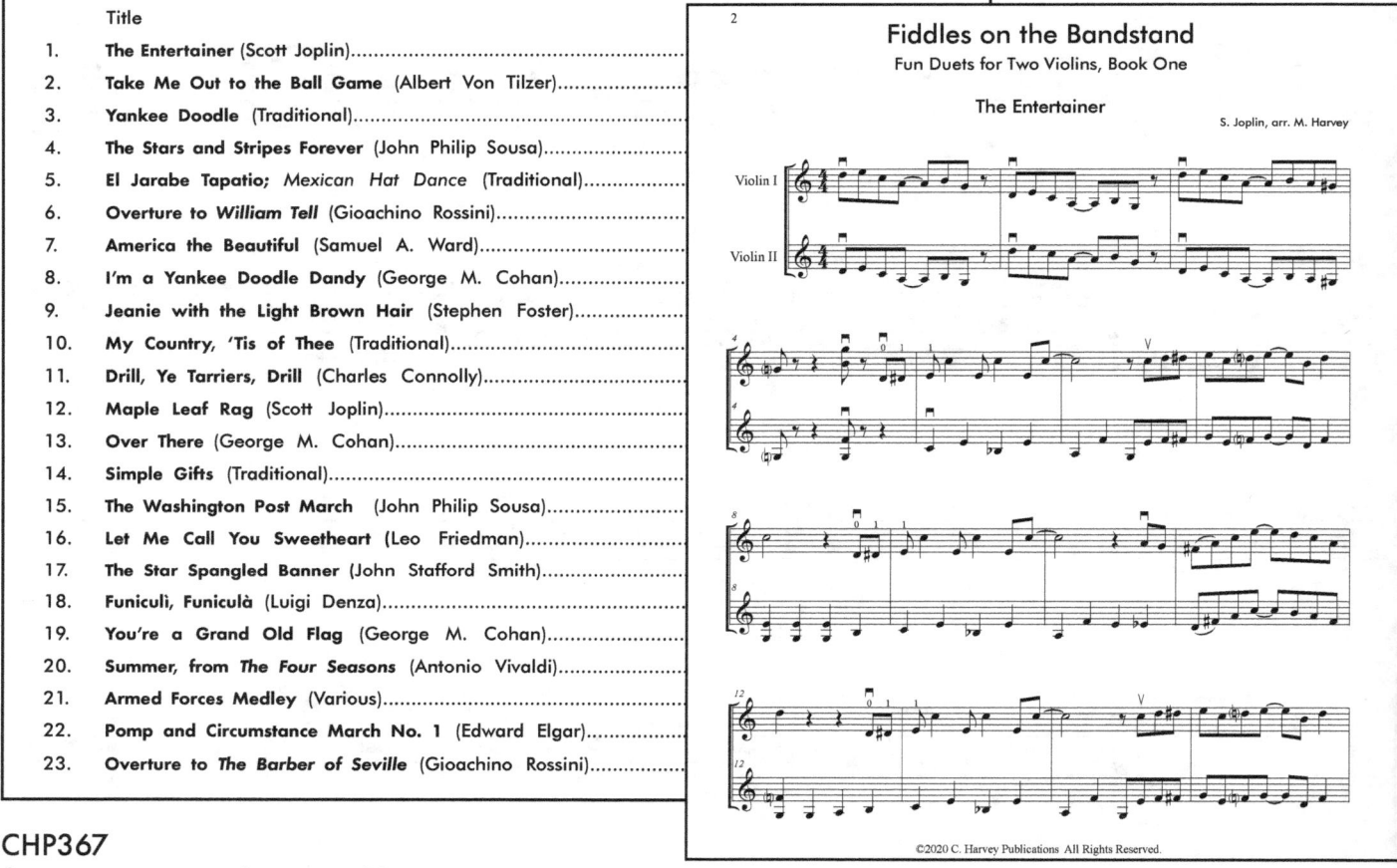

Take a journey to a simpler time when lawn chairs and blankets would be out under the stars and music would waft out from under the eaves of the wooden bandstand.

These are the tunes that got our feet moving, made us smile, and brought us together. Now, with these violin duets, you can bring the toe-tapping, exuberant joy to others and remind us all that through highs and lows, music can be something we share to keep our spirits up and build community.

From Scott Joplin to John Philip Sousa, these violin duets will invite you up on the bandstand, out for a gig, or out on your lawn to play your heart out! Know any violists or cellists? You can pick up a copy of the viola or cello book and play with those instruments as well; the violin book is fully compatible with the viola and cello books.

This violin book is mostly in first position, with occasional basic third position.

Also available from www.charveypublications.com: CHP342
The Bach Double Violin Concerto Study Book, Volume One

Note: The Concerto is broken up into sections in this study book. The complete first movement is at the back of the book.

Concerto by J. S. Bach
Exercises by Cassia Harvey

Concerto
Violin One, Section One: Measures 1-13a

Intonation
Measures 5-6

Key of D minor: B♭

©2018 C. Harvey Publications All Rights Reserved.